FLIES

A TRUE BOOK

by

Larry Dane Brimner

Children's Press®
A Division of Grolier Publishing
New York London Hong Kong Sydney
Danbury, Connecticut

Fly perched
on a flower

Subject Consultant
Jeffrey Hahn
Associate Professor
University of Minnesota
Extension Service
Department of Entomology

Reading Consultant
Linda Cornwell
Coordinator of School Quality
and Professional Improvement
Indiana State Teachers
Association

Author's Dedication
For kids everywhere
who love bugs

The photo on the cover
shows a tachinid fly. The
photo on the title page
shows a black fly.

**Visit Children's Press® on the Internet at:
http://publishing.grolier.com**

Library of Congress Cataloging-in-Publication Data

Brimner, Larry Dane.
    Flies / by Larry Dane Brimner.
        p.   cm. — (A true book)
    Includes bibliographical references (p.   ) and index.
    Summary: Describes the physical characteristics, behavior, and life
cycle of flies and discusses some of the different kinds.
    ISBN 0-516-21161-7 (lib. bdg.)   0-516-26761-2 (pbk.)
    1. Flies—Juvenile literature. [1. Flies.] I. Title. II. Series.
QL533.2.B75 1999
595.77—dc21   99-13836
                                                                          CIP
                                                                          AC

GROLIER
PUBLISHING

1 2 3 4 5 6 7 8 9 0 R 08 07 06 05 04 03 02 01 00 99

Contents

Scorpion fly

Soldier fly

Parasitic bat fly

Bird-of-paradise fly

Black tachinid fly

Male and female mosquitoes

Flies, Flies, Everywhere

More than 120,000 different kinds of flies can be found on Earth. In fact, so many different kinds exist that scientists have not described and named all of them yet. Flies can be found almost everywhere.

Flies have been around for at least 225 million years. During that time, they have become one

of the largest groups of animals on Earth. At least one of every ten animals is some kind of fly.

Some scientists think this number may be even greater because we are still exploring many places. Could these places—our jungles and rain forests, for example—have new kinds of flies that scientists have never seen before? Many experts think so.

Two Wings

All flies are insects. But not all insects are flies. People sometimes call insects "flies" when they are not really flies at all. Butterflies are not flies, for example. Neither are dragonflies. These insects have two pairs of wings, while true flies have only one pair of wings. This is why scientists

7

True flies have one pair of wings.

call them *Diptera*, which means "two wings."

True flies include house flies, mosquitoes, gnats, fruit flies, and many other insects with only two wings. In some kinds of flies, the wings have completely disappeared.

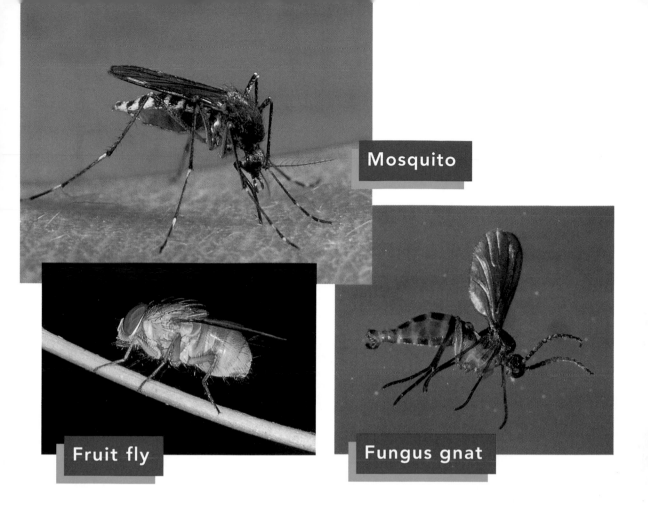

Mosquito

Fruit fly

Fungus gnat

Originally, flies had four wings just like the other flying insects. Over hundreds of thousands years, however, the rear pair of wings on flies

Haltere

A fly's halteres help it balance in flight.

shrank until they became knobs. These knobs, called halteres, shift up and down during flight. They help flies balance.

Flies are amazing acrobats. They can change direction quickly. They can fly backward and they can hover. They can even do somersaults. However, if one of its halteres is missing, a fly buzzes out of control. If both halteres are missing, a fly cannot fly at all.

Up Close

Like all insects, a fly has six legs and a tough outer shell called an exoskeleton. This shell helps support the fly's muscles. It also protects the fly's soft insides like a suit of armor. A fly's body has three parts: the head, the thorax, and the abdomen.

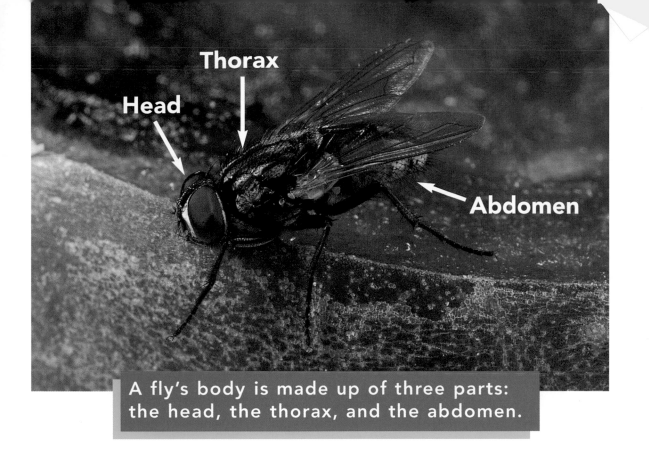

Head

Thorax

Abdomen

A fly's body is made up of three parts: the head, the thorax, and the abdomen.

A fly has one pair of compound eyes on its head. These eyes are made up of three thousand to six thousand facets, or lenses. Each lens is like a separate eye, so

Close-up of a horse fly's compound eyes

flies can see in many directions at once. They can quickly detect the slightest movement. This helps protect them from enemies that might try to sneak up on them.

In addition to its compound eyes, a house fly has three small eyes. These form a triangle between its compound eyes. Scientists think these small eyes help a fly to see while it is flying.

A fly also has two antennae, or feelers, on its head. These

A fly has two antennae on its head.

antennae are covered with hairs that help the fly to smell.

At the very front of the fly's head is a hollow feeding tube called a proboscis. A house fly uses its proboscis like a funnel and straw. Almost everything a house fly eats must be liquid. When a fly touches food with its proboscis, saliva flows down the proboscis. The saliva helps turn solid food into liquid.

The house fly then sucks the liquid through its proboscis,

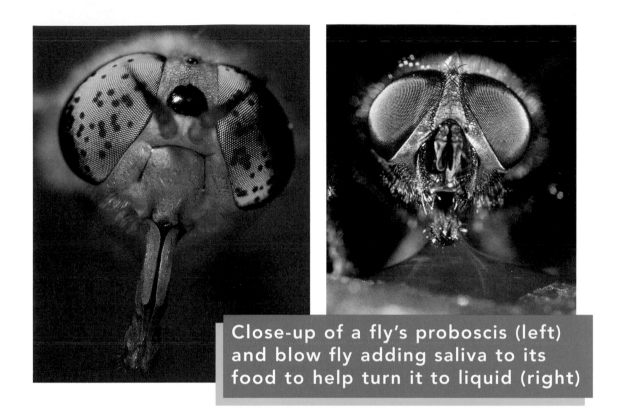

Close-up of a fly's proboscis (left) and blow fly adding saliva to its food to help turn it to liquid (right)

but the liquid does not go directly to the stomach. It gets stored in the crop—a small bag inside the fly—until the fly needs nourishment. Other flies, such as mosquitoes, have mouthparts

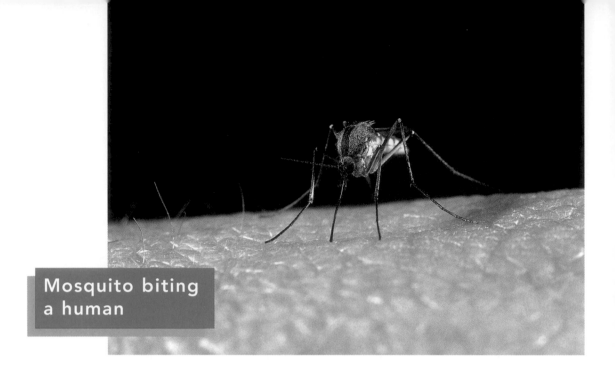

Mosquito biting
a human

that are made to stick into skin.
These flies drink blood for food.

The middle part, or thorax, is
where the wings, halteres, and
three pairs of legs join the body.
The hairs, or bristles, that cover
a fly's middle and abdomen sec-
tions sense changes in the air.

The bristles on a fly's body can sense the movement of air.

This is another way that flies protect themselves. When the bristles sense the movement of air, they tell the fly to make an escape!

A fly does not have lungs like you. Instead, it has openings called spiracles on its abdomen that let oxygen pass directly to

Amazing Feet

Close-up
of a fly's
foot

Fly tasting
a tomato

A fly's feet
are amazing.
Hairs on its feet
help the fly to taste food. When a fly walks on
your dinner plate, it is tasting your supper!

Fly on
a wall

Have you ever wondered
how flies can walk on ceilings
and walls? Each foot is made
up of two sticky pads and
two claws, so flies can stick
and hang on to anything.

The female fly has an ovipositor—a tube for laying eggs—at the tip of its abdomen.

body parts, or organs, inside. A green liquid, similar to our blood, sends nutrients to the organs and carries away waste. If the fly is a female, it has an ovipositor—a tube for laying eggs—at the tip of its abdomen.

The House Fly

The fly everyone knows is the house fly. House flies are scavengers. This means they eat almost anything—human food, garbage, and even manure.

House flies have short lives. On average, they live only about thirty to sixty days.

House flies feeding on a piece of raw liver

During this time, a female can lay as many as 2,700 eggs! However, most female house flies lay between 350 and 900 eggs in a lifetime.

Female house fly
laying eggs

You may have seen two
house flies touching as they
fly through the air. They are
mating. Four to eight days
after mating, the female will
be ready to lay eggs.

Birth of a Fly

Flies change four times on their way to becoming adults. This change, or metamorphosis, takes the fly from egg to adult in eight to fourteen days.

First, a female lays her eggs in or near food—rotting garbage, manure, or even a

House-fly larvae

dead animal. Then larvae—small, white worms that are also called maggots—hatch from the eggs. The larvae eat the food around them and begin to grow.

As they eat and grow, they must shed their old skins. This is called molting. Each time the larvae molt, they are bigger. Their skins harden into tough shells, or puparia, after the last molt.

House-fly larva
surrounded by puparia

Now the flies are pupae.
These are like caterpillars in
cocoons. Inside the puparia,
the pupae change into adult
flies. Three to six days later,

fully developed house flies push their way out of the puparia. At first, they are wet and cannot fly, but they soon dry and fly into the world.

Adult house fly emerging from its puparium

Mosquitoes Are Flies

There are more than three thousand kinds of mosquitoes in the world. Both male and female mosquitoes feed on nectar, a sweet liquid that many plants make. But female mosquitoes need blood to help them make eggs. So female mosquitoes

Close-up of a mosquito (left) and mosquito feeding on nectar (below)

As a female mosquito bites its prey with its proboscis (left), its abdomen fills with blood (below).

bite! A female does this by stabbing the skin with her proboscis and sucking the blood through it.

Mosquitoes need to live near water. This is because their eggs will not hatch unless they are in water. The female of one kind of mosquito lays its eggs on its back leg and then sticks that leg in water so that the eggs fall off.

Mosquito larvae live underwater.

The "Bad" Flies

Many flies are known by the problems they cause. House flies and some other types of flies can spread germs that cause diseases. This happens because they walk on their food to taste it and then land on food that people eat. Other flies, like fruit flies, can ruin a farmer's crops.

House fly feeding on
a piece of garbage

Tsetse fly feeding on a human

Tsetse flies live in Africa. They love to feed on blood. If they bite a human, they can spread sleeping sickness. This is a serious disease that can cause a person to die. Mosquitoes can spread malaria—a disease that causes chills and fevers in people—and many other illnesses.

Flies attack animals, too. Mosquitoes, horse flies, deer flies, and bot flies can make animals miserable and ill. Sometimes the animals become so ill that they die.

Flies bothering a cow

The "Good" Flies

Although flies sometimes cause problems, they can also help us. Some flies make important contributions to nature. Hover flies help spread pollen—a powdery dust inside flowers—from blossom to blossom, just like bees. This helps turn the

Hover flies help pollinate flowers.

Robber fly capturing
a grasshopper

blossoms into fruit and veg-
etables. Robber flies attack
other insects that damage
food crops.

Many flies help clean up
waste. They are important

recyclers because they eat dead plants and animals. They are also food for other animals, such as birds, lizards, and frogs.

Flies are food for many kinds of birds.

Stalk-eyed fly

These acrobats of the insect world may puzzle us, and we may not like some of their habits. But if there were no flies, nature's careful balance would be upset. The next time you see a fly, think about what an important and interesting part of our world it is.

To Find Out More

Here are some additional resources to help you learn more about flies:

 **Books**

Berger, Melvin. **Flies Taste with their Feet: Weird Facts about Insects.** Scholastic Paperback, 1997.

Green, Tamara. **Flies** (The New Creepy Crawly Collection). Gareth Stevens Publishing, 1997.

Miller, Sara Swan. **Flies: From Flower Flies to Mosquitoes.** Franklin Watts, 1998.

Sullivan, D.K. **Do Flies Have Eyes?; A Book about Bugs.** Golden Books Pub. Co. Inc., 1995.

Watts, Barrie. **Fly.** Silver Burdett Press, 1997.

Organizations and Online Sites

Bug Club
http://www.ex.ac.uk/ bugclub/

This is the webpage of the Amateur Entomologists' Society's Bug Club for Young Entomologists, a British club devoted to young people who are fascinated by insects. It provides a newsletter and lists club events.

Mosquito Biology
http://www-rci.rutgers.edu/ ~insects/mosbiol.htm

Info on the biology, life cycle, and habitats of mosquitos. Includes video clips of mosquito behavior.

Most Wanted Bugs
http://www.pbrc.hawaii edu/~kunkel/wanted/

Information—in the form of "mug shots" and "rap sheets"—on the twelve insects that cause the most problems for humans—including mosquitoes and fruit flies.

Young Entomologists' Society, Inc.
6907 West Grand River Avenue
Lansing, MI 48906

An organization that provides publications and outreach programs for young people interested in insect study.

Important Words

cocoon covering spun by the larvae of certain insects for protection while they are undergoing metamorphosis

compound made up of many parts

larva insect in the stage between hatching from an egg and becoming a pupa

metamorphosis process by which a larva changes into an adult insect

nutrients elements of food that keep a living thing alive and healthy

oxygen gas that animals need to take into their bodies to live

pupa metamorphic insect while changing from a larva into an adult insect

puparia rigid outer shells covering the pupae of flies

saliva liquid produced in the mouth that helps break down food

Index

Meet the Author

Larry Dane Brimner is the author of many books for children. His previous titles for Children's Press include *The World Wide Web, E-mail, The Winter Olympics,* and several books about the planets. He spends his summers trying to avoid the biting deer flies in the Rocky Mountains.